HOW TO FIND A NICHE MARKET...

AND MAKE MONEY

M. Morgan

Legal Note: The author of this book has used her knowledge and efforts with the objective of collecting the information appeared in this publication. The information contained in this book has character purely educative; in this sense, if the reader wishes to apply some of the ideas exposed in this book, it will be under his or her own responsibility. The author, in any case, is not held responsible for any direct or indirect damage derived from the use (or misuse) of this book. The information included in this publication is offered in good faith and believing to be exact at the moment of its publication, being subjected to any necessary modifications. This book is not intended for use as a source of legal, business, accounting or financial advice. All readers are advised to seek services of competent professionals in legal, business, accounting and finance fields.

Cover Image:

Author: Cortega9/commons.wikipedia.org.

Table of Content

Chapter 1: Introduction 4

Chapter 1: Introduction 5

Chapter 2: What is a Niche? 9

Chapter 3: What Are the Keywords? 12

Chapter 4: How to Build Massive Keyword Lists 16

Chapter 5: The Importance of the Right Niche 25

Chapter 6: Choose Your Approach 28

Chapter 7: How to Identify a Niche 30

Chapter 8: Commandments of Creating a Profitable Niche 37

Chapter 9: How to Choose a Profitable Niche 40

Chapter 10: Analyzing Your Product or Service 48

Chapter 11: Building a Website around Your Niche 50

Chapter 12: Analyzing Your Competition 60

Chapter 13: Uploading Content 63

Chapter 14: How to Generate Traffic 73

Chapter 15: How to Marketing Your Niche 76

Chapter 16: Be a Blogger on your Niche 90

Chapter 17: Multiple Sources of Income 101

Chapter 18: Conclusion 104

Chapter 1: Introduction

Internet has become the universal encyclopedia that everybody turns to for information and a massive store where users can find anything they are looking for at any time.

Although Internet visitors will rather to have access to free data, they are willing to pay for the right information. Your task here consists in finding out what people are searching for and develop or acquire a product or service that satisfies their wants or needs. In other words, you have to find a group of people of potential clients that have a certain need or a specific wish and who are waiting for a certain product or service.

In order to do so, you need to do some research analyzing the supply and demand of potential niches.

The main reason to choose a niche is that it is a lot of easier to make an impact in a small niche than in a broadly defined market.

Bear in mind that big companies and established marketers are going after mass market while avoiding many small niches that could be available for you to jump into.

Additionally, a small niche is easier to manage and keep update with the new trends in market and you could become an expert in a shorter amount of time, which will be translated into more sales.

If you find out the needs of your customers, they will come to you without much effort and if you also offer them a good service, they will be willing to come back to your site in the future and recommend your products or services to their relatives and friends.

A niche is also a good vehicle to improve position in the rankings of the search engines. For instance, if you open a website related to cars, you will find yourself struggling to compete with thousands of sites for a good place in the ranking while using all marketing tools available and dedicating a huge amount of time to your site in order to avoid that it gets lost in the multitude. However, if you choose a small niche, chances are that you could place yourself in a good position in the ranking, as your competitors are fewer and less possibly less demanding.

The best niches to put your efforts in are the ones that offer the possibility of earning an income for years instead that for months or weeks. In other words, a good niche is that one that is able to attract new customers in addition to previous customers that return to buy from you and they will need to do so for many years to come.

Do not forget that an online business, as any type of business, needs time and effort to flourish. So, do not expect to win instant cash without investing a great deal of time and work in the process.

You must understand that the people who make money online are the ones that put in the extra hour and fight through the days of no sales. You have to decide right now, are you going to be one of the successes or are you going to be one of the people that throw the towel.

If you are looking for a miraculous system to solve all of your financial problems instantly, this guide is not for you. If however, you are willing to put the work in and do not give up that easily, read this book and take action!

Chapter 2: What is a Niche?

Niche marketing has been around for many years and it consists in just narrowing your focus to a small segment of the market. By focusing on a niche you could offer a more personalized service and more experience in the area you specialize in while having to compete with less people.

Knowing your niche market is as important or more than selling your product. The biggest mistake make by most new marketers is to sell their product to everyone and anyone and in the end sell to no one instead of finding their niche and let customers to find it.

When choosing a product or service, you should ask yourself a few questions:

- What type of product or service I want to sell?

- Who would use my product or service and would benefit from using it?

- What solution I offer?

- Is my distribution and shipping process easy and fast?

Remember that the Internet market is huge and niches are everywhere; the problem is that many people simply do not know where to start. The funny thing is that most of good business ideas are in your mind.

Do the research and you can find one or more profitable niches that will make you smile all the way to the bank.

The good thing about a niche is that you will not have to spend your time and effort in trying to attract clients to your product or desperately trying to sell your services at any cost. Instead, as you are offering something that people are looking for, potential clients will come to you without much effort.

A good piece of advice is not trying to compete with the experienced marketers that have already settled down their products and know all the tricks of the business as you are most likely setting yourself up for failure if you try to compete with the established marketers. Instead, be smart and try to offer something else, a new twist that nobody else offers. In other words, be unique and highly specialized.

But before you start the adventure of discovering new niches you must know that on Internet, on the contrary that happens in physical businesses, there is something that will help you to take your message and your product/service to clients: the keywords.

Chapter 3: What Are the Keywords?

Keywords or SEO (Search Engine Optimization) words are those words that are more likely to be search by Internet users and should be included in any text, from article to news passing from websites, writing for Internet.

In doing so, you should use a keyword analyzer such as Word Tracker (www.worldtracker.com- free trial), Wordstream (www.wordstream.com- free) or Google Trends (www.googletrendes.com- free) to have an idea about the words more searched through the search engine. This is free service, just go to the site and enter in a search term and the program will offer a result that will allow you to know if a word is being search by users or not.

These keywords have to be included in every title and headline, in the description of every image included in the website, in the description of your page in your HTML code, in the tags of your source code, in the first two sentences of each paragraph and throughout the text in the same way than a spider net.

The general guideline for creating web content is to write a list of keywords to include in a text and make sure your keyword density is 2 to 6 percent.

For instance, if you have content of 500 words, your keyword should be included 10 to 30 times, mainly in headlines and titles while distributing them in way of spider net throughout the text and being careful of not overdo it or your site might get flagged for spam while your text will lost quality.

A good SEO plan will generate better return on your investment than most other plans.

Therefore, it is crucial to choose the keywords properly finding a balance between highly competitive keywords and those that are not so popular or competitive but still do the job.

Bear in mind that if you use keywords that nobody is looking for, your site will not receive visitors. On the other hand, if you use the right keywords, you will still have to compete with similar sites to attract potential clients. Furthermore, your keywords will have to attract potential clients and not just people who want to have a look at your site out of curiosity.

It is recommended that every time that you are going to add something to your site (a title, an image, a text) you build a list with relevant words and use keywords tools to check their popularity and will suggest you words.

Long Tail Keywords

Long Tail Keywords are sentences composed of three or more words that become a very specific search phrase used by consumers to find products or services that they wish to purchase.

When users want to find information or test the waters, they will usually introduce a single word or two words in the search engine. However, when they are ready to buy their search is more specific and they introduce more words trying to find exactly what they want. These words are known as long tail keywords.

Chapter 4: How to Build Massive Keyword Lists

As keyword marketing becomes more and more expensive and competitive, it has become essential when building your lists to focus on the maximum number of phrases and their variations that a surfer might enter into the search engines.

If you want to attract customers to your site, just follow the same methods than your customers bearing in mind that keyword research is one of the most important steps in the process of identifying and choosing a niche. It can be very time consuming but it will pay a great return if done correctly.

A good way of finding out keywords is to analyze the text to write and develop a list of those words that you think that the users will use in order to search for the information that they are looking for.

You will need to use a keyword tool like www.wordtracker.com or www.googletrends.com, which are free of charge and extremely useful. WordTracker reports results based on a daily search volume. This means that if it shows the number 5 after a keyword that it is searched for approximately 150 times a month.

It is a good idea that you learn to cheat your way through keyword research by visiting sites like www.ezinearticles.com (article directory). By typing your keywords in the search box, you will get some related articles in return and could take advantage of the fact that the author has probably spent hours researching the niche and keywords. Take some of those keywords and introduce them in the keyword tool and then in the search engines to find out how many competitors you will have. In this way and with some luck, you will get a few keywords (10-15) with high searches and low competition.

Once you have your list of keywords, list them in order of daily searches. Since we are going to be dealing with relatively low competition, the number of competing sites does not really matter that much.

Recommended ways to build massive keyword lists:

1. Visit your competitor's web pages and look the title and Meta tags.

2. Search for brand names in Google's Sandbox. This will return additional keywords that searchers entered when using the brand name. You can also enter regular keyword phrases and get related keyword phrases that have been searched on Google.

3. Look over your past customer testimonials and see if there are any keywords you can use. This strategy lets you get inside your customer's mind to produce more market centric keywords.

4. Consider synonyms. Enter your keywords into Roget's Thesaurus for a list of related synonyms or visit www.lexfn.com.

5. Think of singular and plurals keywords.

6. What about verbs? Example: Ride, rode, ridden, ridding, rides.

7. Use hyphenation and variations. Example: off-shore, offshore, off shore

8. Consider domain names. Many people enter domain names into the search engines rather than their browser address bar. Example: in July 2004 cnn.com was searched 633677 times.

9. Get books on your subject and use the terms in the index and glossaries to grow your keyword lists.

10. Use keywords tools. It helps you find all keyword combinations that bear any relation to your business or service.

11. Use abbreviations and misspellings. A good misspelling tool is Search Spell. Search Spell uses actual misspellings entered into the search engines.

12. Use acronyms. An acronym is a word formed from the initial letters of a name. Example: due diligence becomes DD.

13. Combine your keyword phrase into one word. Example:

- Strawbale houses => strawbalehouses.

14. Use "space" and "+" with keywords. Example:

- Strawbale+houses

As you go about your research do not forget to be on the look for low competition keywords to target. For instance:

How to

Remove

Fix

Help

Solve

Solution

Symptoms

Comparison

Cure/Treatment

Relive

Relief

Buy

Repair

Training/ Train

Do not be afraid to use this list as a start your own research but remember that this is just the tip of the iceberg in terms of frequently asked questions and there are thousands of questions and problems that people are searching for information to.

How do I become a movie extra?

How to get art scholarships?

How do you take a digital photo with a specific size and resolution?

What I should know before buying a used car?

How to sell a used car?

Is Botox safe?

Are breast implants safe?

How do I get rid of excess hair?

What causes Cellulite?

How to grow and build a home business?

How to start a non-profit organization?

How to write a business plan?

How much money do you need to start your business?

How does an online business owner file for taxes?

How to earn money blogging?

How do I get more traffic to my website/ blog?

Is microwave cooking safe?

What is the average cost of college today?

How to deal with kids bullying each other in class?

Are private schools better than public schools?

How accurate are IQ tests?

How to make money in the stock market?

How do I train for a marathon?

How to build up muscle mass?

How do I start my own Bonsai garden?

How often should you replace a roof?

How do you get a reference from your current boss?

What is copyright?

How is a copyright different from a patent or a trademark?

How do I download music for free legally?

How to learn to play the piano?

How to tune a guitar?

How to buy a house after bankruptcy?

How do I get over a past love?

Can a long-distance relationship work?

What questions should I expect on a job interview?

How to write a resume?

How to write two-week notice letters?

How do I get over my fear of public speaking?

How to handle stress?

How do I write my own book?

What is the best way to promote a novel online?

Chapter 5: The Importance of the Right Niche

Choosing the right niche can make a huge difference between earning a few dollars and making a more than decent income. A good advice is to choose a niche that will last in the long-term instead something that is in fashion now but it will be no longer use or searched for in a few years. One of the best ways of finding out whether or not a niche has a long life is by to look at its history through the search in the keyword tools and have a look at the history of similar sites.

The main characteristic of a niche is that you will find yourself in direct competition with a lower number of similar sellers. This means that you should offer something unique and different that will send you away from your competitors.

This could be quality, speed in the delivery, an extra bonus or extra information, money back guarantee, 24 hours customer service, free shipping, etc.

One of the most common mistakes made by new online marketers is to pick the wrong market. Invariably many of them find themselves promoting a product or service that has a low demand or, on most occasions, has a huge number of competitors most of whom are more experienced that the newcomers.

The result is that they invest a considerable amount of time, effort and money to obtain just a few monthly sales.

Make sure that there is a market and a need for the product. Ideally, you should have some knowledge on your niche (it is not totally necessary) as you will work more and in a more productive manner if you have an interested on your niche. Once you establish your first niche and get some experience it will be easier to create and develop the next one and obtain benefits.

Chapter 6: Choose Your Approach

When you wish to look for an appropriate niche, you should take your first decision: choose a niche based on a product or choose a niche based on a certain audience.

If you choose to focus on a product, a good piece of advice is to sell what people are already buying! The idea is to identify the gaps in the market, and build your niche around them. In this way, you will not compete with many and large sites because you specialize. For instance, find out what kind of books are online users looking for and they cannot find. If you find that out, you could become an authority for books on a particular area.

Another way you can build a niche around hot-selling products is to give them a twist by customizing or personalizing them.

You could sell personalized gifts or something similar as the product based niche is based on spinning off existing markets and trends.

On the other hand, the niche based on audiences is focused on special interests or information. You begin by identifying broad areas of concern like health and finances, and then drill down into subtopics like, for example, allergies or credit repair.

Next, you dig further into the subtopics, letting the product come to you. When searching an audience-based niche, you start off with zero preconceptions about what to sell not having a product in mind. This is the model preferred by most e-book authors and information marketers.

Chapter 7: How to Identify a Niche

The first step to identify a profitable niche in the market is to take on board a brainstorming session. This will help you generate a list of potential markets to research if you are starting at ground zero with no ideas or to put your ideas in order if you already have a product or audience where to focus.

1. Write down a list with your interests, abilities, knowledge and strengths. You need to analyze your own interests, abilities, knowledge and strengths before you begin. This analysis will help you to narrow down the market quickly. If your passion is music, for example, you know there is an almost endless supply of potential products and potential buyers in areas as diverse like instrument sales, vintage instruments, techniques and lessons memorabilia or instrument repair, among others.

Besides, you will know that any or all of those can be tailored towards: solo artists, bands, fans, managers, engineers, agents, etc.

2.- Revise your entire life and daily routine writing down everything you know and have done. Go one step further and ask your friends and relative to let you know about their skills and abilities. A combination of both things will proportionate you a long list of possible niches.

3.- Scan your bookshelves to see what reference books you have and to some online research. Revise articles that you have read in magazines or courses that you have taken in the past.

4.- Pay attention what people talk about their hobbies and interests and identify the trends on the market. The markets are in constant change and with those changes new problems and solutions arrive like new diet plans or new technologies which can become new business opportunities.

Study the holes in the market to find out the trends that are not still covered and search for new solution to old problems. Ask yourself if there is room for individual needs that are not being covered and if you are able to address those problems from a different angle.

5.- Check some magazine on your chosen niche. Have a look at the highlighted classified ads and ask for the information brochures. Over five to six issues how many of the adverts are repeated? If they were not making money the ads would not be running. Check up how long the brochure takes to arrive and what they are selling and honestly think if you could improve the quality of what they are offering.

6.- Do some online research based on your lists. Hop over to eBay to research all the different sub-categories. Which ones are active? Which ones are commanding high prices? Also, check the forums related to your potential niche.

Research what products or services have a low competition. A good idea is to have a look at "how to" or "how" pages as those sites offer a great amount of information on different products and services.

You also can revise the best popular online and check their categories.

Finally, visit www.Amazon.com to check out if there is a niche on your chosen product; verify who are the top sellers; get ideas of what is selling; try to find where there is a gap that you may fill and read users' feedback.

7.- Use keywords to find out whether or not an online market exists and whether or not people are searching for your possible product or service.

When you do this it, you could can across three different situations: confirmation that your niche idea is viable and deserves further market research; negation of your original idea because no one is searching for what you want to offer; or revelation of untapped niches as if you start from scratch, you could spot potential niches in the keyword data.

Bear in mind that it should be at least 25000 searches for a keyword in order to consider a possible niche as productive. Therefore, if you are look for a product related to music guitars, for instance, a set of good keywords to search for could be: strings, picks, solos, repair, second hand, etc. As results, you will come across many words that could be paired up with "guitar": guitar strings, guitar picks, etc.

And then, use a few words of sentences: "guitar chord chart", "how to play guitar", "learn to play guitar", "left handed guitar"?

8.- Scan the news, open your eyes and mind to opportunities, paying attention to what you listen on the bus or you see in public advertisements.

9.- Find out how other people are making money to known whether or not the niche is profitable. It is all right if you have a few competitors, but if the number is really high change your product, as you will waste your time in a market that will only give you a low income, if any.

10.- Choose the type of product or service that you want to offer. If you want to sell an e-book, you could certainly write a "how to guide" on guitar repair or how to play guitar, as long as you give it your own unique twist.

But if you want to sell hard goods (or create a different kind of information product), then you will to look further and consider something like: custom guitar pick, customized guitar pick, create your own guitar pick, etc.

The market is clearly interested in customization and personalization and if you manage to create this type of product you will have plenty of customization-happy guitar players beating on your door.

11.- Focus on something specialized instead of trying to sell something that many other competitors already offer. For example, if your business is focused on e-books, to avoid competition with hundreds of sellers you should specialized your books in, for instance, outdoor sports and you will find yourself competing with a reduce number of sellers.

Finally, remember that you will have to spend days, if not weeks, in doing your search so you could find niches that other people are neglecting.

Chapter 8: Commandments of Creating a Profitable Niche

There are a number of "sacred commandments or principles" to bear in mind at the time of initiating the search for a productive niche:

1. The Principle of "Adaptation" - Copy successful examples in another business or industry and trying to adapt them to your own business, product, or service.

2. The Principle of "Addition" - Add something extra to your product or service that your competitors are not doing.

3. The Principle of "Combination" – Ask yourself what positive elements can you combine from another product or service to make yours better.

4. The Principle of "Customization" – Personalize your entire product or part of it, as buyers love that personal touch that makes a product exclusive and unique.

5. The Principle of "Easier" – Make your product or service easier to buy, use or adapt in order to attract more clients.

6. The Principle of "Elimination" – Ask yourself if you could eliminate an inconvenient with your product or service by offering less risk, less pain, less waiting, etc.

7. The Principle of "Longevity" – People do not like to invest their money in things that do not last. So, make sure that your product offer some feature that makes it last longer.

8. The Principle of "Reversal" – Reverse the products or services offer by your competitors. For instance, if they target young people, you should target seniors.

9. The Principle of "Safety" - Show others how your product or service can add safety or reduce risk. People hate to experience loss, feel insecure, or waste money.

10. The Principle of "Speed" - Today more than ever people hate to wait. Try to find a way that you could offer a faster service or product that gets faster results or solves customers' issues faster.

11. The Principle of "Yucky" – It is said that the secret to success is to be willing to do what most people do not want or like to do. So find out what people do not like to do for several reasons and charge them to do it. If you offer something that your competitors do not want to do for their client, you basically get potential clients out of them.

Chapter 9: How to Choose a Profitable Niche

The first thing to bear in mind is that you cannot expect that your success will come completely out of the blue. You should neither expect a great deal of support from your relatives and significant others who will probably want you to get a 9 to 5 job with a regular salary. Some of them will probably want to start their own business, but they do not find the courage to do so. This means that they could be critical secretly hoping you fail, so that they can justify their own fears and insecurities about being entrepreneurs. Therefore, it is fundamental that you stay focused and positive.

Do not forget that the any business requires an investment to take off.

Even if an online business could be cheaper than a physical one, at one point (sooner than later) you will need to invest some of your benefits in software, outsourcing and different tools while giving learning all the new trends in the market.

A profitable niche market is the one that has enough potential customers and it is not dominated by established businesses.

When you decide your niche, develop a search and learn everything that you need to learn. An example of what a niche market is "Women who play golf who want to learn how to drive the ball longer and straighter" instead of "People who want to learn how to shoot better scores in golf" as there are far too many people within the main category (golf) and basically everyone will want to shoot better scores. One more example is not to focus on "Fishing" and instead target "Fishing Baits" or "Fishing Lures" both of which have a much more specific focus and so on.

Once you choose a powerful niche, you should decide how to turn it into money. In doing so, you need to decide if selling physical products producing and selling your own products or buying them wholesale and sale them at retail; offering services such as web design or consulting; selling digital information products like e-books and reports or making money through advertising or affiliate programs. You could use one of these options or a combination of them, as there is no reason for you to limit to just one type of product.

Test your products by offering them on a blog related to your niche at a very low price or for free just for a few days.

In doing so, you will know whether or not your product or service could be successful while building a database of potential clients and obtaining some testimonial and valuable insight into the strengths and weaknesses of your service or product.

When deciding which product is right for you, there are a couple things that you can look at:

- Visit a website of affiliate marketing like www.clickbank.com and have a look at the products they offer there and which of them are the ones that sell.

- The next step is to look at the search engines to find out whether or not you can find many sites that offer free information about the products that you have in mind. If that is the case, choose another product, as people will not buy your product when they can find it for free. If however, there is not a whole lot of free information, but enough for you to research and get information for articles and other advertising, you probably found a good product to market.

- Have a look at the sources that affiliate pages could grant you for free like articles, graphics, free reports, list of profitable keywords and other information that will help you in marketing their product.

- Ask yourself if you have options with you chosen product keeping in mind that there is more than likely than another person selling the same kind of product.

Remember that not every niche is profitable and that choosing the wrong niche and your chances of success go down by ten times. So, when you are doing your search to spot out niches bear in mind that if the online market is too small to sustain a business it will not be profitable and, therefore, it is not a niche!

Bear in mind that the search does not let you know what types of customization people are looking for and whether or not those searchers can actually turn into buyers.

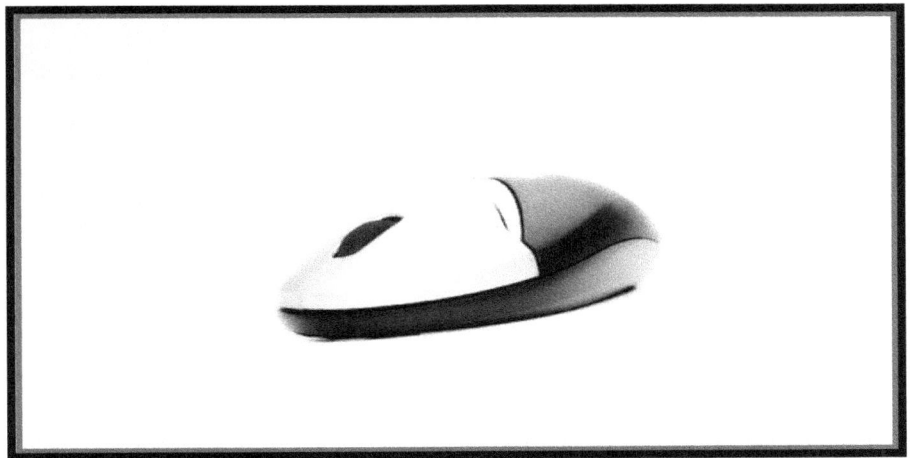

The problem here is that the results of keywords searching are not really good at answering vital questions for a future business. Instead, keyword searching gives you a snapshot of trends.

In order to find out all the information that you need to know before setting a business, you need more advanced research tactics. At this point, you will need to enter your keywords into the searching engines.

It is often difficult for beginners to distinguish between healthy competition (a certain amount of competition is good as it is a sign that the market is solid enough and that people are buying and the niche is profitable) and market saturation.

To know whether your market is profitable or not you need to weigh your keyword(s) search volume against the number of "hits" or indexed pages reported by engines like Google.

So, for instance, if your niche keywords receive an average 500 searches per month, while Google reports that it has indexed 550,000 web pages containing your keywords, you potential market is saturated.

On the other hand, if you find a niche with very few competing web sites or sponsored listings, you may be facing an uncovered or a 'dead market'.

To check out whether you have an uncovered niche that could grant you great profit or a dead market, a good idea is to elaborate a survey and kindly ask people to participate in forums related to your niche and maybe offer a freebie for participating in the survey and leaving an email address. Through a survey you will know what people are looking for, how much they will be willing to pay and whether your niche holds any profit potential. Once you have your answers, it is time to rule out your chosen niche or to create a product or service for your niche market. Before you start, you need to determine the best format for the product.

Chapter 10: Analyzing Your Product or Service

Once you decide if your future product is viable or not, you will have to analyze your product and to your competitors in order to decide which is the best manner of presenting your future product to your potential clients. In this way:

1. Think in deep about your product/service to find ideas.

2. Do not be too critical or judgmental, as it will slow down the creative process.

3. Keep the session light, loose, free spirited and do not forget your sense of humor.

4. Write down your ideas.

5. Set a minimum length of time or amount of ideas to obtain from each session as establishing goals will help the process while avoiding never end sessions.

6. Write down the problem, the goal, or the subject at the top of a piece of paper like, for example, "Ways to Attract More Customers". Write down every idea (good or bad), as the target is to get as many ideas as possible.

7. Next evaluate the most do-able ideas and take action.

Chapter 11: Building a Website around Your Niche

The first step to attract clients to your website is to develop a site that is easy to access and navigate. The good news is that there are several options available in order to create a site as you can create it yourself using HTML coding, a word processor, an HTML editor or the easiest of them, blogs like Wordpress. If you use a word processor or an HTML editor, you can create a site using a template or the tools within these programs.

HTML Coding

HTML is a programming language used for building websites and which is generally easier to learn than other programming languages as everything is conveyed through a series of tags and attributes.

HTML is easy enough to learn through a book or an online tutorial. However, if you want to create more powerful websites, you'll want to learn how to use scripting languages in conjunction with HTML.

Word Processor

Most modern-day word processing software such as Microsoft Word or Word Perfect can create HTML documents.

You would design the webpage as you would any other document except you would save it as HTML, a web page or any other similar option given by your word processor. Depending on how recent your word processing program is, you might even be able to design your website using a 'web layout' view. This view is more reflective of how your web page would look in a browser, making it a better choice when creating your website.

The negative point is that websites created with word processors tend to display oddly being really difficult to fix everything properly and necessary to invest hours and hours of editing to obtain a more or less decent result. In this case, the only option out is trying to keep the site as simplest as possible. Think that it is better a short but nice website that still fulfills the objective of making money that a large and unprofessional sit that could discredit yourself and your product.

HTML Editor

HTML editor programs are designed to help you create or edit HTML, without having previous knowledge of HTML. The most famous and used HTML editors are Dreamweaver and Microsoft Office FrontPage. They are more expensive than word processors (except FrontPage) but the final result is more accurate.

Templates

Website templates can be used in word processor and with HTML editors being an alternative for those who do not have the time and/or knowledge necessary to design the graphical elements of a website.

There are literally thousands of free templates available and equally effective than a paid one but with simpler designs. You can also find affordable templates in sites like www.e-Bay.com.

Another alternative is using templates from your web hosting company as usually these templates can be used through a separate editor from within your web hosting account. You can also find web-hosting companies like Yahoo Stores which are specialized in the creation of online stores, allowing you to build an e-commerce site similar to the ones of www.amazon.com or www.buy.com.

Pre-Made Website

Another option is to purchase a pre-made website which is ready-made sites with the graphical layout and the content developed. Use web hosters like Homestead (http://www.homestead.com), Joomla (www.joomla.com) or Dupral (www.drupal.com) but there are many good point and click web site builders out there.

Wordpress

Wordpress is maybe the most popular software to set blogs as it has some good advantages like the fact that it is free of charge while it offers a great number of gadgets, which are very easy to set and use and are able to transform your page into a highly professional website. Additionally, Wordpress does not require any technical or computing knowledge as everyone can set his/her own website just by following a few simple step described in the blog.

If the idea of building a website looks too complicate to you or you have not enough time to dedicate to this task, think about hiring the services of a professional web designer.

There are some good websites where you could find freelance web designers and writers like www.elance.com, www.fiveer.com or www.getafreelancer.com.

General Tips

The first thing to bear in mind when it comes down to website design is keep your layout simple. Most effective websites have their logo and banner advertising on the top, links to other websites on the left side and content on the right side or links on both the left and right sides with the content in the middle.

Be careful with the colors and the layouts, combining soft colors that do not cause headaches or refusal to visitors and inserting easy and simple layouts that allow people to find the information that they are looking for without getting lost in the pages or spending several minutes wandering around.

You should create eye-catching and descriptive titles and structure your content in such way that invites people to read, using multi-media content that offer a fun experience to visitors.

Remember that if your visitors have a pleasant experience, it is very likely that they will return every time that they need some information or acquire products/services.

It is essential that you include and regularly updated content as you will not only providing information for your potential clients but also will give search engines the chance of finding keywords easily.

A good piece of advice is to ask friends and relative for their honest opinion on your website before you focus your efforts on attracting traffic. Once your website is perfectly set up, it is time to increase your page visibility, this means to be able to place your site in a really good ranking position.

This means that when you search for a website through a searching engine like Google (you should work preferably with Google it is by far the most demanded searching engine) the results obtained after a search that is the ranking.

If you site is located in the first or second page of the results displayed, you are doing your job properly. Bear in mind that when people look for something on Internet, they invariably will have a look at the first results displayed by the search engine. So, it is crucial that your website be located in the first positions.

A good idea to optimize your site is visiting the top-ten sites related to your niche and analyze their content, keywords and its location within the texts, as well as, the links used in those sites. Also, get some design ideas like colors, testimonials and features on the sites. You might pick up some good ideas to improve the look and feel of your own website but being careful of do not committing plagiarism.

Also, it is important to upload the new page every time you make a modification, as it will attract search engine to new content. Even so, it is a good practice to check your ranking monthly as search engines change their algorithms often.

It is also important to have Google material on your website, links to YouTube, a Gmail address, a Google map of your business and a profile on Google+.

The reason to use Google content is that right now Google is the most powerful search engine and if you use its products, they will set your site on a good position.

When you are ready to check your page rank, you can do it for FREE with the Google PageRank Report and focus your efforts on improving your result in the search engines.

Chapter 12: Analyzing Your Competition

Knowing to the competitors is essential when you are working on developing a niche site, as it will help you to build a more competitive site for yourself. The first thing to do in order to analyze your possible competitors is to introduce your keywords in the search engines using quotation marks. Then, have a look at the next factors:

- The kind of sites that are ranking high and how strong they are. Visit their websites and try to find out what products or services the offer and how much they sell.

- The number and type of Adwords campaigns that are being run.

- The number of competing sites that could be found with and without quotation.

- If when introducing your keywords, you get a result of a few hundred (even a few thousands worldwide) and some Adwords Ads running, that keyword works really well. You are going to want to go through this process for each of the keywords that you have compiled.

- Pay attention to how the websites look like, colors, layout, images, type and size of articles, etc.

- Then, check at the links that come and leave the websites ranking on the top and check whether or not those links offer good content.

- One of the best indicators to use is http://www.bing.com/toolbox/webmaster as you will be able to find out exactly how many links the site has coming in and exactly where they are coming from.

- Consider your strengths and weaknesses in relation to your competitors. As you go about your research look around at your competitors in your niche and try to find out what they are offering. You should ask yourself whether or not you can fill what they are not offering and make a profit doing so.

- Contact the masters of websites that offer similar or complementary (but not the same) products to yours and offer them the change of developing a reciprocate promotion and granting access to each other databases. In this way, you will turn your competitors into business partners to give a more complete offer and obtain more visibility.

Chapter 13: Uploading Content

Now that we have our niche selected and the keywords that we are going to attack picked out, the next step is to create some content to generate traffic and attract clients.

There are two ways of creating content: by doing it yourself or by hiring the services of professional outsourcing.

Remember that quality is better than quantity and that, especially when we talk about online business, eighty per cent of the sale is done by an eye-catching design. So, it is hugely important that your product has a highly professional design and a really catching sales letter.

In order to create your product, you need to create content, especially is your product are e-books.

You need to create content for any product as, at one point, you will have to set a website and a marketing campaign to promote your services. This will require time, effort and certain abilities as a writer.

Visit sites like Yahoo Answers and search for variations of keywords with the end of knowing what problems people are facing and what kind of solutions are offered to them and what extra something you could offer. If you pay close attention you'll pick up a couple of great titles for articles and a list of different things that you can write about.

To get content, you can include news, articles, multimedia, links to articles, e-courses, information on products, video tutorial, webinars, etc. You can also open a forum so people can participate and include content themselves.

Ideally, to have enough content you should write an original 600-word article and 3 rewrites of that article plus 2 unique 300-word articles and 3 rewrites of each of those 2 articles. Writing articles and submitting them to article directories is a simple, but very powerful and effective way to create interest and generate traffic to your site and, it is FREE.

Through article directories, you submit an interested and original article that people could use for free in their websites or blogs. In exchange, there are required to display your name and website, including a link to your product/service/website, while leaving the content unchanged.

You may think that you are doing the job for others but actually, a single article of yours could be on display on several blocks so, you could attract more readers who, if feeling interested in your article, will link to your website.

When submitting an article to a directory, you should be a number of aspects in mind:

- Use original and fresh content. You can create the content yourself but if you think that you do not have enough time or talent to write an article from scratch, you always can use PLR (Private Label Rights) content.
Just decide what you want to write about and search for the issue on Google adding the words PLR. For instance, if you have decided to write about weight loss introduce in Google, weight loss PLR. PLR content PLR is free and varied and sometimes you could come across high quality e-books, reports or articles.

When using PLR, you will have to rewrite around 70% or 80% of the content to create an original article. This means, you could use the idea but changing the content, as PLR content should not be modified and it should be offered with the name and link of the original author.

Do not try to use the PLR article as it is as it is very likely that other person has already use it and your article will be refused for being duplicated. Besides, you will have to show the name and link of the original, which means that you will be generating traffic to the site of that author and not to your site.

- Read some articles in any directory on your niche topic and get ideas for new articles. Public domain repositories offer free material like software, books, music, designs, images, etc. that are very useful when creating an innovative article. Just search for public domain on Google.

- Elaborate articles related to the services or products that you are promoting on your website. In this way, you will attract to your web, people who are interested in that particular niche and, therefore, the chances of obtaining potential clients will increase.

- The articles should be around 300-500 words in length and be keyword optimized. The articles should be interested and linked to your products or services, offering information and providing solutions but avoiding turning them into mere promotion letters or they will not be published.

- If you are selling a book or e-book, write an article related to the issue exposed in your e-book, informing people and offering solutions while adding a sentence like "if you need more information, find a book on the subject in the next link: your website or link of your product".

- You can find out what they are looking for in your niche by using any keyword generator. A good idea is to offer new solutions to old problems we all share like a how to remove a stain on your child's clothes or how to fix a stuck drawer.

- Be creative and your articles will be appearing all over the Internet. If you have a humorous story about how you discovered the solution, add it to the article.

- The most successful titles are those that include a number ("How to Lose Weight in 4 Weeks"), offer a solution ("How To...") or solve a mystery ("The Secrets of...").

- Create a new list of steps to get something done, as people love handholding and step-by-step lists of techniques or processes to make their life easier.
- Remember that every article directory has different submission guidelines that have to be followed or your article will not get published.

- You can hire an articles submission service, which for a fee will submit your articles to hundreds of directories. However, they will not bear in mind the submission guidelines for each directory, so you could get refused in some of them.

- Some popular article directories are: www.ezinearticles.com/, www.articledashboard.com/, www.articlecity.com & www.articlemarketer.com

If you have more money than time to invest in product creation, outsourcing your product creation to a ghostwriter or freelance writer can save you time and headaches.

You can often find top-notch writers, artists and programmers letting their services go at bargain basement prices because they need projects like yours to build their portfolio and reputation.

The best pages to find high quality outsourcing are: Elance (www.elance.com); Rent a Coder (www.rentacoder.com); ScriptLance (www.scriptlance.com) and Fiverr (www.fiverr.com). These sites attract a huge pool of freelancers and protect both providers and clients by providing escrow services.

When you post a request for bids on one of these sites, you have full-control over whom you choose to complete the work and what you are willing to pay for it.

Ask for samples of previous work (and references if possible) and ask the freelancer to sign a formal written non-disclosure agreement that will include an acknowledgement clause through which the freelancer rescinds all claims to copyright upon accepting payment for the completed work.

You can also search locally for college students or part-time workers looking to trade skills for quick cash.

Chapter 14: How to Generate Traffic

Once you establish your website, it is fundamental to focus your efforts on improving the ranking of your site on the online search engines. In order to do so, include new content almost every day. You should upload a large article of quality once a week and short news or posts on a daily basis. You also can upload videos or images as multimedia content, which is able to generate a great deal of traffic. Do not worry as it is not necessary that you create all the material needed on your website as you could "borrow" images and videos from pages like YouTube.

You must know that the main source of traffic is found in article directories like http://www.ezinearticles.com and on social platforms like www.facebook.com-, www.twitter.com-, www.digg.com-, or www.boardreader.com where your message will reach thousands of users.

The key to generate traffic is to present yourself like an authority. You could do this by entering in forums related to your niche and participate by offering solutions. You could also visit sites like http://answers.yahoo.com and find some questions that relate to your niche. Make sure to answer the questions like you are genuinely concerned. Little by little, add a comment like: "if you need some more information, you could visit my blog or site".

By doing this continuously, you will generate a ton of traffic and even a few sales. This is especially true because you are offering a solution to their problems and you are building a reputation of expert, so they will trust you and buy from you. Use software programs like www.uniquearticlewizard.com to upload your posts to hundreds of sites in a few seconds, allowing you to rank better and faster. You will need to invest some money and, therefore, maybe a good idea is to wait for a few months before signing for a software program.

Chapter 15: How to Marketing Your Niche

In order to make money with your site, you will need to drive people to it. In order to do so, you will have to:

Became an Expert in Your Niche

Sign up for forums and blogs related to your website. Visit them regularly and post, answer questions and offer solutions. It is also crucial that you keep learning constantly in order to be in touch with the new trends in the market.

After introducing yourself as a new member with a brief and friendly post in the category set for the occasion, create a signature that appears at the end of every post, email or private message you may send. The signature may include your name and the link to your site and may be one or two brief sentences.

A carefully constructed signature is viral and will zip around the Web.

Read the rules of the forum and find out how it works and its categories while knowing the moderators and what the most popular members write about. The next step will be to get active and participate in the forum asking questions and offering solutions.

Offer links to free resources or offer your own products for free (a report, an eBook, etc.) and win the trust of other members little by little.

In doing so, you are building reputation within the forum which is essential to go through the next step: initiate you're the marketing of your website.

If you just join a forum and try to self-promote straight away, nobody will buy your products or services because members of the forum do not know you and trust you. Besides, it is more than probable that you will be "invited" to leave the forum.

To success in a forum, you have to build a reputation as an expert before offering your products and services subtly. Instead of selling directly, just offer a solution and then add a sentence like "if you need more information, visit this website: name of your website".

You can also consider the possibility of creating a discussion board or a forum on your own website to boost interactivity among your visitors. Visitors who have had a good experience on your discussion board will return when they have a problem to solve or just for the social aspect of it.

Furthermore, if your visitors are satisfied with your product/service or content, you could encourage them to let others know about and forward your free articles or newsletter, which will include a link to your site. This provides additional exposure and it will increase your database of potential clients.

Communicate within Your Niche

Because consumers have become smarter and have more options between which to choose, it is indispensable to build a good relationship with your visitors and clients through newsletters, freebies and useful articles.

Offer trustworthy and valuable information and they will back to you when they need to know something else or you need a solution to a problem.

Create a Unique Domain Name

This will make your site look more professional and trustworthy to visitors. Use BuyDomains (http://www.buydomains.com) or Nameboy (http://www.nameboy.com).

Turn your Competitors into Business Partners

Turn your competitors into allies by complementing each other. For instance, if you find blogs related to your niche, some of those web masters will be willing to post your articles and let your site known to his or her readers.

You can also find another entrepreneur that offer products in your own sector but in a different area. By offering him a link exchange program you could get access to each other's customers and benefit mutually. Exchanging links with other web site owners is a must if you want to improve your search engine rankings as the search engines consider your site more relevant if it contains links to and from other sites.

A good and free site to use to find credible web sites to exchange links with is Linkmarket (http://www.linkmarket.net).

Build Mailing Lists and Client's Databases

E-mailing list is a cheap and effective way of keeping in touch with your clients and offering them an incentive to come back. Emails can be easily personalized thanks to software programs and are very low-maintenance.

The key here is to build a strong database of clients and future potential clients.

You can do this through jumping into a joint adventure with another Webmaster who targets the same niche than you but in a different capacity and ask him/her to promote each other to your clients. In this way, the database of both websites will increase with the clients of both sites.

The faster way of building a database is to offer something for free. This could be a report, webinar, software program, e-book, etc. and ask visitors to introduce their name and email address to crap the freebie.

You can also ask fellow webmasters and bloggers to offer the free item to their clients.

Another option is to find Facebook and twitter accounts specialized in the field of your e-book or report and ask them to offer the freebie to their followers. In this way, you will increase your database while generating huge traffic to your website.

You also can build a long database of present and future clients through a joint adventure with other pages related to your niche but that offer a slightly different product or service to yours. Contact with the webmasters of those pages and ask them if they will be interested in a reciprocate promotion and an exchange of databases.

Use Video Marketing

Use video-sharing platforms like YouTube or Metacafe to boost your online marketing campaign.

A link back to your website can be placed in the description of the video to funnel traffic back to you and do not forget to put links at the bottom of the video and at the end of the video during the editing process.

Sign Up for Affiliate Programs

Affiliate marketing is when you promote another company's website, service or product in return for a commission which is usually given when a sale or lead is actually made from your advertising methods.

There is also de possibility of receiving commissions for click, this means that if the URL of a company received a click through an advertising placed on your website.

In both cases, the URL of the company contains a special coding that would trace back to your affiliate account and, therefore, they know when a sale or lead is received through your website or advertising.

Join some affiliate programs like www.amazon.com, www.ebay.com, www.bestby.com, www.commissionjunction.com-, www.clickbank.com- or www.associateprograms.com.

There are also many other sites that you could find through some research on the search engines. Bear in mind that if the site is not in the first pages of results after an engine search, it will not be profitable or have a good reputation.

Just type your niche title plus the word affiliate among comas and write a list of ten programs that you will find. Then, research through the programs to find out which one of them is profitable.

If none of the pages offer an affiliate program related to your niche, contact the web masters of some of the sites that you have searched for and introduce your product or service to them.

Perhaps help them set up an affiliate script and share in profits actually, if there is no affiliate program in that nice, you and that company can make benefits.

Include Google AdSense Ads

Google has a great program for web site owners who wish to make a little extra money for simply displaying Google ads on their web site. It's easy to sign up and free. Just visit Google (http://www.google.com/ads) and sign up for their AdSense program.

They'll give you some html code to copy and paste on your site. While Google decides which ads will actually appear on your site, you can decide how the Google ads will look – choose colors, borders, etc. and where to put them on your pages.

Include Pay-per-click Advertisements

This service works by displaying a list of advertising on your site and giving you a commission when someone click on one of them. This commission can range from as low as $0.01 to as high as $100 depending on the company, though most of the time you will earn just a few cents.

Usually, large insurance companies are the ones more willing to pay the best commission per click and you could get a decent amount if you manage to have a decent number of legitimate clicks (clicks from genuine visitors).

However, bear in mind that the search engines can detect when someone is doing irregular clicks and that is considered a fraud, which means that not only your affiliate program will be over but that you can also have serious legal problems.

Regarding approval, you have to follow a similar process to the one required in affiliate marketing website, although pay-per-click sites are usually less strict and it is more than likely you received an approval. You would show as many advertisements from other income streams as you want, always that your website offers interesting content for the visitors.

Syndicate Your Content

Another free marketing tool is the "Really Simple Syndication" or RSS. This process is a kind of feedback that you produce on your website. You can select part of your content and create a kind of diary that people registered to your website will receive in a similar way to a newsletter.

The selected content, which could be anything from articles to promotions or updates passing from special events, is added to an RSS document and then registered with an RSS publisher or aggregate.

If you are technical enough, there are a number of software programs that will help you in your task. Otherwise, you always could hire the services of a freelance who do the job for you.

The key to success is to create useful content, bearing in mind your target audience, as RSS is an easy and free way of releasing news and press release.

At the moment of publishing choose the specific category to reach your intended audience and avoid categorizing yourself into a hole. If your content can be useful or interesting to different audiences, submit it to different aggregates under different categories.

Create Unlimited Pages

Each time you have published new content in text, audio or video, you're system will automatically create a new webpage. And then, there must be no limit to the numbers of webpages you can create.

Direct Selling

In context selling of relevant products and services on your content site is relatively easy, as the audience attracted by your content is the best fit for what you sell.

Offer Resale Rights E-Books and Reports

Many of them are free and you could sell them for a few cents without spending time and money in the product.

Offer Paid Products

Instead selling your products, you could offer your visitors the chance of using it by paying a small fee.

Chapter 16: Be a Blogger on your Niche

Niche blogging is a practice that has become more and more popular in the last years as it is inexpensive and you will be saved regarding shipping and customer services. Additionally, blogs are, in general, low-maintenance and you only need to upload your template and post your updates.

There are two points to bear in mind when building a niche blog: that the blog needs constant updates in order to attract and engage visitors and that a niche blog should be narrowed enough to attract a targeted market.

To set your blog you could use platforms like www.blogger.com or www.wordpress.com but bear in mind that most of these providers do not allow advertising of any form or restraint them.

This means that it will be very difficult for you to monetize your site. Furthermore, the ones that allow advertising, like Wordpress, have the right to change the terms and conditions of their service at any time.

Another option is to get your own domain and web hosting and pay the hosting bill. You will have more control over your blog while being able to set all the advertising and affiliate programs that you wish.

At the time of designing your blog, you should keep focus on your niche and look as much professional as possible. Your design should be consistent throughout and you should check your grammar and spelling and the use the SEO words that will help you to rank your site.

By setting up a blog around that niche having the following advantages:

(a) Join Communities

MyBlogLog (www.mybloglog.com) is a social networking platform that builds communities of bloggers and allows them to have a MyBlogLog calling card featuring their own avatar or picture.

Featuring the MyBlogLog widget on blogs is a good way of knowing who dropped by your blog, and also allows others to see you when you leave your calling card somewhere.

Leaving comments also encourages people to do so on your page, and by returning visits to those who visited you, you encourage them to notice you as a 'good' presence.

(b) Interaction

Blogs allows interaction between you and your readers, as well as, allows your visitors to post their comments, thoughts or opinions.

Constant interaction with your readers builds a feeling of community and trust.

Once the relationship is there, you can then recommend products while your readers and subscribers will be more ready and willing to accept your product or services.

(c) Increase Search Engine Ranking

Search engines have a software program called 'bot' (known as spider) that searches for new content to include it in the rankings.

Basically what this means is that the more frequently you update your site, the more frequently the search engine 'bot' will visit your site, and this helps to boost your search engine rankings. If you make postings and publish regularly to your Blog, you can be sure that search engines will visit your Blog again and again. You can then place links of your other websites in your Blog and the search engines will index these quickly.

Building Niche Blogs with Wordpress

Among the available platforms, maybe the easier, most complete and professional is Wordpress.

Besides it counts with a number of advantages as you can easily:

(i) Create a content rich niche site just by copy, paste and publish your content immediately or schedule it for auto publishing at a later date.

(ii) Get search engines to crawl your site instead of wasting time with search engine optimizations. Wordpress has a 'secret' built in feature, that if activated can get search engines to crawl your site like crazy.

(iii) Broadcast your niche blog to thousands of other sites hungry for new content related to your niche market.

(iv) Manage your content easily through the use of 'categories' and 'subcategories'.

(v) Link all pages together automatically.

(vi) Increase your search engine ranking for targeted keywords you want by activating a Wordpress function.

(vii) Change the layout and look of your blog through the use of 'themes', attracting visitors and making them stay.

(viii) Insert Google Adsense or sell products from affiliates with the click of a button.

How to Drive Traffic to Your Blog

There are many ways you can drive traffic to your blog like create different categories that include powerful keywords in such as way that it will allow you to upload more content and attract the search engines more often.

If you keep building your site with keyword-rich articles, eventually you could have hundreds of pages linked to your categories and each of those links will use the anchor text of your most important keywords.

As a result of all those internal keyword-rich links, your site will end up ranking very well in the search engines.

During the first month, it is recommended to add at least a short article or multimedia content on a daily basis as it will attract a lot of traffic and the search engines spiders to your blog.

The next step is submitting your blog to the various blog directories in the proper categories.

Then, use a Ping Service, which consists in sending a notice or 'ping' to the major directories every time you add a new posting to your blog.

Having the ability to actively 'ping' an update message to all of the major directories means that search engines no longer need to regularly visit blogs to discover new changes.

In this way, the new content on your website is presented to the public in a more timely fashion whether you rely on search engines or social bookmarking websites for your traffic.

The best independent ping servers are www.pingomatic.com and www.kping.com. You just have to type in your blog URL and Pingomatic will send your ping to Yahoo and about 15 other large directories. That will bring the spiders back to your site almost immediately!

If you use other free service like Blogger.com, you need to manually ping blog directories to let them know you have an update. However, with Wordpress you need not do so as every time that you publish a post, as it will automatically ping the sites you have listed.

Another way of attracting traffic to your blog is through a RSS Service. By submitting your new blog to these directories, you can start getting traffic almost immediately. Quite often these feeds will result in a lot more traffic than all the major search engines combined. This is why it makes so much sense to build your niche site as a blog. You can have twice the traffic, and get it much faster than with a static site.

One of the top RSS directories you should submit your site to are: www.masternewmedia.org/rss/top55/.

Once you have submitted your blog to the directories, you can get it indexed by Yahoo almost immediately by adding your RSS feed to your My Yahoo page. Just visit www.yahoo.com and click on the "My Yahoo" link to set up a free account.

Then, click on "Add Content" and add the URL of your blog RSS feed into the "Find Content" box. Your new site should be indexed in Yahoo in just a couple of days.

If you have an RSS feed, you can have it included in Yahoo and MSN and your website will be immediately listed in these major search engines within 24 hours!

These, besides the fact that a blog is able to attract traffic twice as fast than a website, are the main reasons to choice to build a blog.

Chapter 17: Multiple Sources of Income

Remember that there are many other sellers competing with you and that if you have only one site and your competitors take over the market, you may lose all of your income. But if you have 4 or 5 sites and your competitors take over one of your fields, you still will have 75% or 85% of your income through your other sites.

In other words, it is a good idea to have more than one source of income each different web site would generally be a different business. They could relate to each other, but not necessarily.

During the months that your business is building, you could be looking for other ideas and set a second website. Over time you have other great ideas.

The main issue here is to control costs: the cost of advertising as well as the website costs and shipping fees (if that is the case) and build a database of clients for each product or service that you offer.

Having different income streams is a must on today's online world if you are serious about making your living from an online business. Internet Marketing today has become much too competitive, and the newcomer has very little chance of breaking in. Different niches with their own websites and relevant content are the best solution.

In brief, you need to search and find a profitable niche; develop suitable products/services; set up a blog/website and several social profiles; to some online marketing and repeat the process over and over.

Imagine having a niche site that generates $20 a day and around $7300 a year. Now, ask yourself how many sites could you set up and run bearing in mind that time and effort that you need to put in the process. Maybe, working hard and keeping your websites updated, you will manage to set up 4, 5 or 6 websites focused on 4, 5 or 6 niches. This means between $29200 and $43800 a year.

Before you realize it, you will have a few niches that are generating a nice profit every month.

Chapter 18: Conclusion

Internet has changed the way in we consume and, therefore, the way in which should target our possible clients developing different marketing strategies.

The Net offers amazing chances to capitalize your ideas and to set up a business that could grant you enough money to cover some of your bills or even to be able to win a more than decent monthly salary.

Internet gives the possibility of get any product or service with just a click of a mouse. Many people find shopping online addictive because you can look for the best prices and pay straight away from the convenience of your own home.

But not only clients benefit from the current online culture. The home business owner can also benefit from today's market culture.

Just as consumers can shop from their living rooms, business owners can manage business from their own homes.

The advantages are many: getting rid of bully bosses; saving quite a lot of commuting time; establish your own and flexible timetable and having more time to spend with your family and friends as you can dedicate to your love ones the time that you save from transport.

One of the ways of being successful online is focusing your efforts on a niche as providing specialization to a reduce market you can get a small piece of the pie.

The great thing about having a niche business is that you are not struggling to compete against established marketers.

The next step is taking action, create a business plan and move forward. Do not become one of those people who get information, buy books and acquire knowledge and then do not implement that into their business idea do not progressing from where they are now to where they want to be.

It is not necessary to hold university studies on website design as building a website is easier than you may think. Just do the research; let the niche market dictates you the product or service that you need to create; develop a product or service to satisfy the niche's customer requirements and start selling while keeping learning and aware of new trends in market.

But remember, spend the time and energy to research, evaluate and test your idea for a niche before your settle your business idea and do not make the mistake of developing your product before you take on board some research on its viability.

You should neither forget that any method not matter how good it could be, would not work unless you will be willing to do take it into practice. After reading this book, you have all the information you need to get started in this fascinating world of online niches. Now, you are the only one who can make it happen as no one else can take action for you.

Reading through this book is the first step but not enough as buying a product does not guarantee you profit. Therefore, work hard and put your ideas into action with the end of reaching positive results and do not forget this: do not compete, be genuine!

This is your year!

Index of Illustrations

1. Idea. Author: thetaxhaven/www.flickr.com.
2. SEO. Author: BWDCanada/commons.wikipedia.org.
3. Search Engines. Author: FindYourSearch/flickr.
4. Online World. Author: Rodolfo E. Aristimuño/commons.wikipedia.org.
5. Computer Mouse. Author: Trostle/www.flickr.com.
6. Domain. Author: Rock1997/commonswikipedia.org.
7. Content. Author: FindYourSearch/www.flickr.com.
8. Writing Articles. Author: The Italian Job/commons.wikipedia.org.
9. Twitter. Author: Rosana Ochoa/www.flickr.com.
10. Communities & Forums. Author: Cortega9/commons.wikipedia.org.
11. Blog. Author: Cortega9/commons.wikipedia.org.
12. Ping Symbol. Author: jb2.0/www.flickr.com.
13. Marketing Online. Author: FindYourSearch/flickr.

www.ingramcontent.com/pod-product-compliance
Lightning Source LLC
Chambersburg PA
CBHW051728170526
45167CB00002B/844